THE
SCHOOL
OF MUSIC

WRITTEN BY MEURIG AND RACHEL BOWEN
ILLUSTRATED BY DANIEL FROST

WIDE EYED EDITIONS

Welcome to the School of Music

STUDENT'S NAME

_____

Contents

20–21 LISTEN UP!

Why should we keep our ears wide open?

SCHOOL OF MUSIC

LEARN

CREATE

LETTER OF ACCEPTANCE
TO THE
SCHOOL OF MUSIC

CONGRATULATIONS,

PLEASE JOIN US ON THE
FIRST DAY OF TERM,

The School of Music

School of Music

Dear Student,

Welcome on board! The inspiring people at the School of Music have come together to guide you through 40 lessons. In Term 1, we will introduce you to a wide range of music, and musical intruments, too. Some of them might be familiar, while others might not! Look out for the musical sign ♫ – wherever you spot this, you can listen online to recordings from some of our favourite musicians.

In Term 2 you will learn about the basics of melody, harmony, pitch and rhythm, and you will be shown how to read and write music. In Term 3, you'll also discover that there are lots of ways to get involved, whether you prefer to write music, listen to it or perform it. Try out each of the activities to better understand how some of the ideas and theories work in practice.

We can't wait to get started and are looking forward to the first day of term…

Why should we enrol at the School of Music?

MUSIC IS GOOD FOR YOU

Music is good for your brain. Listening to it, and in particular making it, makes your brain fitter and livelier.

Music is good for your body. It's brilliant exercise. You become a champion musical athlete. You breathe better. You tone and strengthen muscles. You become better coordinated.

Music is good for your social life and the way you feel about yourself. Lifelong friendships are made, and it gives you greater self-confidence.

Last but not least, having a deep and widespread appreciation of music makes you feel more intensely. You are more in touch with your emotions and – as if it is almost a 'sixth sense' – music triggers strong memories and sensations like nothing else.

It might seem like a bold statement, but we all think music makes you a better person!

WHAT CAN - AND WILL - THE SCHOOL OF MUSIC DO FOR YOU?

The School of Music opens up your ears and ignites your imagination. By introducing you in the broadest possible way to music's power and potential, you will be inspired to step further along your own musical journey – whether as a listener, a performer or a composer. At the School of Music, we set some little musical fires burning; and if you tend to them with hard work and passion, those flames could become the most wonderfully warming fiery furnace for the rest of your life.

There is a wonderful world of music out there – one that tells us through its captivating web of sounds a wider story of human civilisation. Love and war. Joy and sadness. Struggle and hope. History, geography, language – maths even. It's all there in music. To such an extent that, although some people think music lies out on the edges of educational need – an optional extra, a nice thing to have if there's the time and money – we at the School of Music think it's absolutely, fundamentally, enjoyably at the blazing centre!

WHAT CAN'T THE SCHOOL OF MUSIC DO FOR YOU?

Unfortunately, there isn't a book in the world – not even this one! – that on its own can turn you into an amazing violinist, singer or guitarist. No single book can create, just by the pages being turned, mini-Mozarts or singer-songwriter millionaires.

If this book could do that, we wouldn't be music professors. We'd be music magicians – really really rich ones, living a glamorous, lazy life on cruise ships and ski slopes.

So who's in charge around here?

MEET THE BOSS!

Some people call me The Maestro, others call me Herr Direktor. (It depends what they had for dinner – spaghetti or frankfurters). I have been in charge here for just over 25 years – they threw me a very fine party to mark the occasion.

WHAT DO I DO?

I am the very eminent and grand Head of School – just that little bit more eminent and grand than any of my staff. I am a first-rate conductor of first-rate orchestras, choirs and opera companies, and the artistic director (in some of my not-very-much spare time) of a super-duper highly-regarded music festival. Everything about me is top notch, so I think you'll agree I'm the perfect person for the job!

HAVE I ALWAYS BEEN SO IMPRESSIVE?

Oh no! It hasn't always been chauffeur-driven cars from the airport and Royal Gala concerts. I grew up in modest circumstances, and was raised alone by my mother. Right from the start, she made me appreciate the importance of self-discipline and hard work (and a good night's sleep).

HAS IT BEEN MY TALENT ALONE THAT HAS MADE ME SUCH A SUCCESS?

Through my love of music, the world opened up for me at school and beyond. So although you wouldn't guess from my wonderfully polished and grand exterior that I started out further down the ladder, I've never forgotten where I came from, and I always make sure I work very hard. You can say 'the more you put into something, the more you get out of it' about a lot of things in life – and this is never more true than with music.

HOW IMPORTANT IS THE SIZE OF A CONDUCTOR'S STICK?

Once upon a time, conductors used to use very long sticks (we call them batons) to keep a large orchestra or choir in time. But it isn't necessarily the case that the bigger the orchestra, the bigger the stick: in fact, one famous Russian conductor uses a tiny toothpick as his magic wand, and other conductors don't use a baton at all! I like to think that my brilliance as a conductor comes from my natural sense of authority and leadership, the subtle expressivity of my body language, the focus of my rehearsals and – of course – my high level of charisma. Charisma is charm, magnetism and earning potential all rolled into one.

IS IT POSSIBLE TO LEARN CHARISMA?

Unfortunately, my friends, it isn't. It's something you either have or you don't. If you have it, you'll certainly know – things will happen to you that don't happen to other people. Regard it, like I have all my life, as the most precious gift. It will get you far – alongside hard work of course!

IS IT ALL ABOUT ME?

Goodness me, no! How could you possibly think that?! There are lots of other talented and lovely people at the School of Music. Turn the pages to meet some of them.

What does it take to make a star singer?

NICE TO MEET YOU

I am Diva Venus, the dazzling opera star. (Some of you may have heard of me already!) My glamour might be a little overwhelming when you first arrive at the School of Music. But don't worry, I'm just a pussycat really – with a very loud purr.

WHICH IS MY MOST POPULAR CLASS?

I'm pleased to say that my sessions on 'How To Perform, Make An Impression and Get Your Audience Coming Back For More' are always packed out, and have been live-streamed to more than 30 countries.

IS DIVA MY REAL NAME?

Absolutely! I was baptised that way. And I've always been happy to keep my family name too. Neither of my two lovely husbands – one after the other you understand – had names that would have worked with Diva. I'd have either become Diva Donaldson or Diva Weever.

DO TRAINED CLASSICAL VOICES HAVE ONLY LIMITED APPEAL?

Actually, my glittering profile means that I'm famous far beyond the opera house and concert hall. I'm a regular at major sporting events, belting out national anthems through the stadium's enormous public address system before a major league baseball match or cup final. I'm always a hit on TV chat shows, too.

WHAT COMES FIRST? THE BIG VOICE OR THE BIG PERSONALITY?

They say I'm larger than life – like opera stars are supposed to be. But I'm only 65 kilos. I checked this morning.

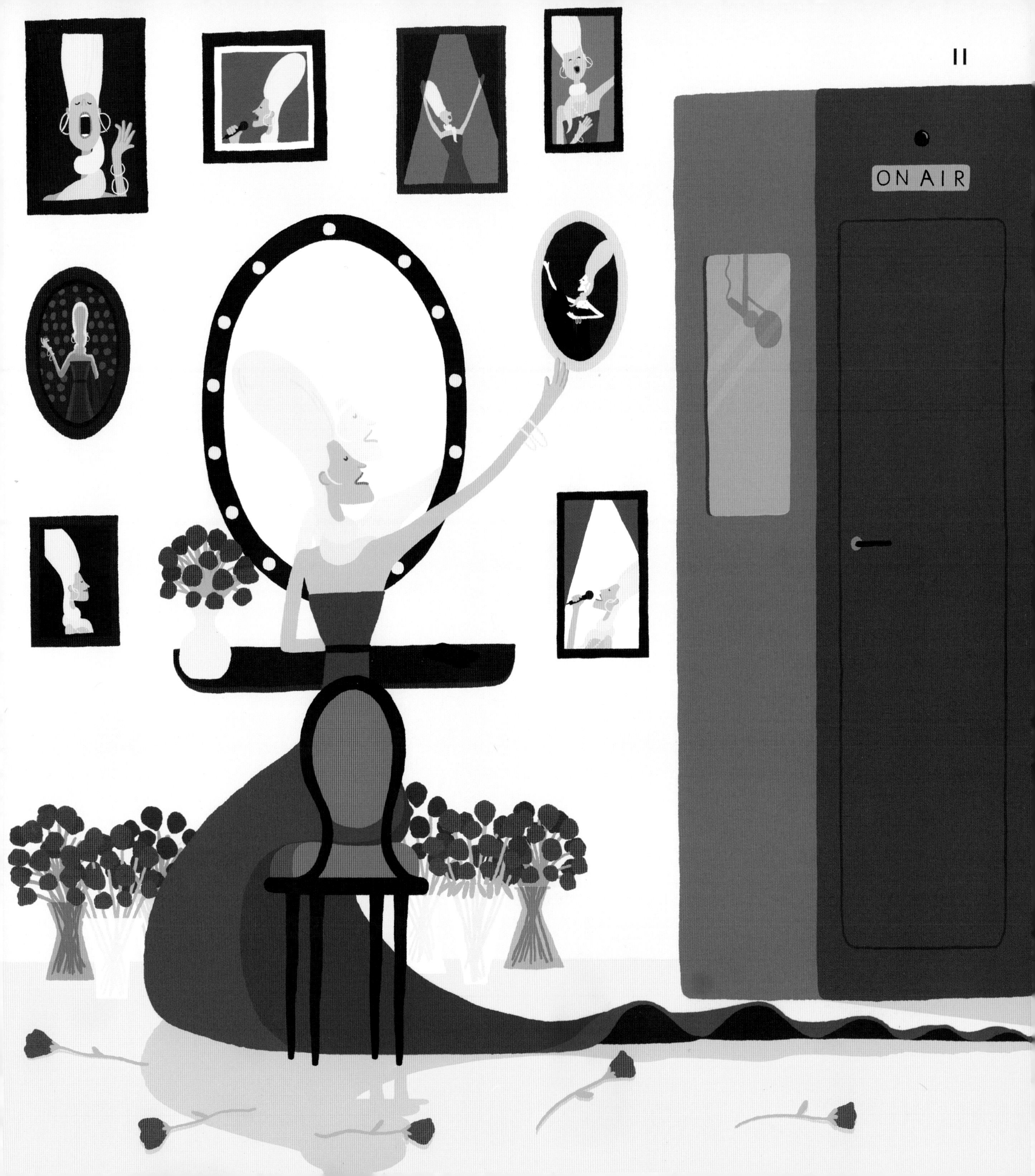
ON AIR

How do an instrumentalist and their instrument get along?

BUONGIORNO! SALUT! GREETINGS!

I am what a major national newspaper described a few years ago as a 'globally significant' cellist, and I am the School of Music's Head of Strings. I like my students to address me as Signor Vibrato.

VIBRATO - THAT'S A PRETTY UNUSUAL NAME

Well, I have to be honest, it's not the name I was born with. I decided that it would be useful to have a name that related to my chosen profession. After all, once upon a time, Mr Baker was a baker, Mrs Carpenter was a carpenter and the Butcher family were all butchers. Vibrato is the Italian word for a rapid, subtle variation of pitch. Players of stringed instruments, like my cello, achieve this by quickly moving their fingers on the fingerboard.

DID THE NAME CHANGE ASSIST ME IN MY INTERNATIONAL CAREER?

Yes it did! No other cellist is called Vibrato, so I have always stood out in a crowd, or on a concert poster. It worked a treat. But I have had a busy, globetrotting life because I am a pretty good cellist, too. When I play at my best, I am one of the best.

FLYING AROUND THE WORLD SOUNDS GLAMOROUS...

It does, doesn't it! But cellists have to buy a seat on the plane for their cello, too! Stringed instruments are very fragile, and even though the cases we put them in are strong, it's too risky to put them in the aircraft hold along with all the suitcases. Apart from anything, stringed instruments don't like extremes of temperature, and it gets very cold in a plane's luggage hold 10,000 metres up in the sky. Sadly, there's no discount from the airlines for my cello not guzzling the free food and drinks on board.

WHAT ARE MY TOP TWO CAREER MISHAPS?

Once, I managed to leave my extremely valuable Stradivarius cello in the back of a Brussels taxi. How silly of me! We got it back just in time for my concert, and the publicity generated on Belgian TV was fantastic. When I walked on stage at the start of the concert, my cello and I got a standing ovation.

AND THE OTHER ONE?

On another occasion, I was playing solo Bach in front of the Queen of England and my G string broke. It was quite embarrassing, but she was very understanding.

Why is it best to be busy, fit and adaptable?

GOOD DAY, NEW STUDENT!

People tell me I'm so busy and so capable in a range of jobs at the school that I never quite know how to describe myself! But first and foremost, I am the Director of Studies, and I keep everything in perfect administrative order. When Professor Trunk is away on other musical business – which is quite often – they just call me The Chief.

HOW MANY DIFFERENT BALLS DO I NEED TO KEEP UP IN THE AIR?

Rather a lot, so it helps that I only need a few hours' sleep every night. Aside from all the meetings I attend and all the timetabling I do, I teach organ, piano, composition and yoga. Oh, and I run a dance class for older people in our local community called Zimmer Zumba. There is no reason why you should stop dancing when you start needing a walking frame. It is very successful, and an important additional source of income for the School.

HOW MANY INSTRUMENTS CAN I PLAY?

At the last count, it was a little over 20. I try to learn a new one every year, and I'm making good progress with the bassoon at the moment.

ORGAN OR COMPOSING – WHICH IS MY FAVOURITE?

When I play the school's thunderously loud organ late at night, with no-one else in the building (apart from Ronny upstairs, of course), there is nothing more thrilling. I really do pull all the stops out, and the floor shakes! But I love the creative buzz I get when I compose music, too. I write for film and TV as much as for concerts. I am a practical, no-nonsense kind of woman, and people like asking me to compose things because I always deliver on time!

SO WHY YOGA IN A MUSIC SCHOOL?

Musicians have to be very fit. They have to be in peak condition, both in their heads and in their bodies. Playing an instrument or singing is a very physical business, and all that practice can make musicians' bodies tense and badly aligned. So yoga is a good way of helping with this. I am one of the bendiest, fittest people I know.

Just how creative and exciting can music get?

WELCOME TO MY HOME!

I am the School of Music's composer-in-residence. Yes, literally so: I can't afford my own house or apartment, so I really appreciate living for free in the attic.

WHAT DO I TEACH?

I am the best person to tell you about how to write your musical ideas down on the page. You'll be seeing a lot of me in Term 2.

AND WHEN IT'S JUST ME ON MY OWN IN THE ATTIC?

I like to compose most of all, and I dream of my compositions being performed not just once, but twice and three times too. Alongside my teaching at the School of Music, I have a parallel existence playing guitar in a range of tribute bands. Tribute bands are a way of keeping pop and rock music alive when the original band members are either dead, or too old or lazy to perform their own music anymore. It's best not to be in a tribute band of a band that has just re-formed. They fill stadiums, but we only fill smaller venues like clubs.

HOW DO I COPE GOING FROM CLASSICAL CONCERTS TO POP AND ROCK GIGS?

My musical tastes are impressively broad – one of the pieces I'm working on is a children's opera called *Rapunkzel* – and when I climb into the musical costumes of The Upbeatles, Fabba and Some Direction, I always remember why it pays to keep your ears and eyes open.

AND WHAT ABOUT ALL THOSE WIGS?

I lost my hair when I was quite young (that was a bit careless of me, wasn't it?). So when I'm playing in the tribute bands, it's great to be able to dress up the top of my head as well as everywhere else. See Lesson 38 for my history of music in hair.

How can percussion instruments bring the world together?

HI THERE!

I'm Roxy. And though I wouldn't want to bang on about it (do you like what I did there?!), lots of people say I'm the most versatile and irresistibly cool teacher at the School of Music.

SO WHY DO PEOPLE THINK YOU'RE SO COOL?

Well, it might be my very long hair, my fabulous dress sense and the infinite bendiness of my body when I'm performing. But it's also, I think, because being a percussionist allows me to make so many different sounds – and when I'm really going for it, to make SO much noise.

TELL US ABOUT ALL THOSE DIFFERENT SOUNDS

My garage at home stores every percussion instrument you've ever heard of, and some that you haven't. They come from all corners of the globe, and so do I! I'm a quarter Venezuelan, a quarter Korean, a quarter Danish and a quarter Sri Lankan. Christmas is always interesting when my grandparents get together!

DO YOU FIND IT HARD TO KEEP STILL?

Rhythm runs through my veins, and I am positively twitching to tell you all about it – from quavers, crotchets and rests to bongos and backbeats (see Term 2).

THERE'S NOWHERE TO HIDE AS A PERCUSSIONIST IN A MUSICAL TEXTURE. DOES THAT WORRY YOU?

It terrifies me! If you Crash, Bang, Wallop in the wrong place, everyone notices! And if you start slipping out of time, everyone starts slipping with you. My recurring bad dream is that I fall asleep playing the side drum part in Ravel's *Bolero*, and the whole of the orchestra gets very cross with me.

IT LOOKS LIKE A GOOD WORKOUT. DOES BEING A PERCUSSIONIST KEEP YOU FIT?

Like many of my colleagues at the School of Music, I eat and drink a lot – I need to, because of the calories I burn up banging drums. And yes, I think that I'd easily win a School of Music arm-wrestling contest.

Why should we keep our ears wide open?

There is an awful lot of noise in our modern world – the constant intrusion of engines, machines and electronic beepery.

We hear it. We get used to it. Sometimes our brains are clever enough to block it out.

Noise is the badly-behaved brother of sound. Sounds are all around us, all the time. Noise has an unwelcome habit of blocking out the sounds of nature, the sounds of silence. Except that even in the quietest, most serene places, there is never total silence. In that 'silent place', there will always be the exquisite chirruping of a bird, the distant bubbling of a stream or – if you are unlucky – the overhead crackle of an electricity pylon.

Our ears are amazing things. Our brains take in so much information from what our ears enable us to hear. But there is one thing better than hearing – and that is listening. Hearing can be something that happens to us, whereas listening is something we make happen – it is an active and engaged thing that our ears and brains properly take part in.

Term I at the School of Music is all about listening. Music, like noise, is all around us nowadays. In fact, when it flows into our ears uninvited, it has the potential to be, quite simply, noise. But if we learn to be really good listeners, and really open-minded listeners, then we give ourselves the gift of appreciating music in a much deeper, multi-dimensional way.

'Open-minded listening' is really important to us at the School of Music. As you will see on the following pages, there are so many different kinds of music, that people tend to define themselves by what they listen to. Music generates its own tribes and clubs of belonging, and that is a great thing in itself. Except when people close off their minds – and ears – to other kinds of music that don't fit with how they define themselves musically.

Country music fans might say they hate hip hop. Heavy metallists might not be drawn to gypsy jazz. Give it all a go, we say. And with the newfound skills you have acquired in the School of Music, you will at least have listened in a way that allows you to work out why you don't like something you don't like. Quite a few people think Western classical music is too 'highbrow' for them – they think you need to be a member of a very exclusive club, or of a certain age, to understand it or enjoy it. We at the School of Music think they are wrong! Although we do recognise that a certain kind of longer attention span needs to be acquired for longer pieces of music. And when something is more complex or lengthy, the more you listen to it, the more you hear in it.

In Term 1, always with the aim of inspiring you to listen well and listen widely, we will introduce you to the widest variety of music, from across the centuries and around the world. Then we will show you how music has evolved over many hundreds of years, and how humans have ingeniously invented various ways of making it: instruments that are blown, hit and plucked, instruments played with keyboards and bows, and of course the most ancient and universal of all instruments, our singing voices. Finally, we will demonstrate how music doesn't just exist in its own little corner of life – how it connects wonderfully with film, dance, theatre, mathematics and with architecture.

So, turn the page and let's begin!

Lesson 1

What different kinds of music are there?

Music is just music – right? Well, yes… but no! As Head of School, I feel it my duty to teach my students that music comes in all sorts of shapes, sounds and sizes. One piece of music sounds different to another. That's one of the amazing things about it – each sequence of musical sounds has its own unique character, just like no two snowflakes or fingerprints are the same.

So how do we deal with that infinite variety? How do we describe it? Somebody once said (rather brilliantly) that "writing about music is like dancing about architecture". They were saying it's kind of missing the point – you listen to music, just as you look at or live in architecture. But in the same way that we have names in our different languages for colours or items of clothing – giving us words to differentiate between green and blue, between socks and crop-tops – we have developed a language to describe music. And, most usefully, to describe different styles of music.

Niagara and I decided a few years ago that the School of Music needed to capture all the musical styles in one place. That way, all our students would be able to see and hear them all together as equals. We put on a fundraising concert to pay for the conversion of our bottom floor, and I was given the enormous job of creating our Great Basement of Musical Pigeonholes. When you 'pigeonhole' something, you categorise it, you put it in its designated place. So come downstairs with me and see my collection…

ACTIVITY

Choose some styles of music here that are unfamiliar to you. Search online for examples of each of them and have a listen. Which ones do you like the most?'

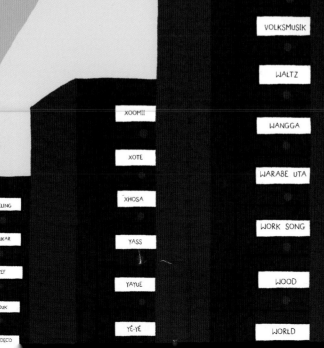

VERISMO

VIDEO GAME

VILLANELLA

VOCAL JAZZ

VOLKSMUSIK

WALTZ

XOOMII

WANGGA

XOTE

WARABE UTA

XHOSA

WORK SONG

YODELING

YASS

YUKAR

WOOD

ZEF

YAYUE

VALLEN

ZOUK

YÉ-YÉ

WORLD

ZYDECO

TRI

TR

TRO

TU

TUR

TUVAN SIN

TL

TWO

UNDERG

VALLE

VAUD

MUSIC COMES IN ALL SORTS OF SHAPES, SOUNDS AND SIZES

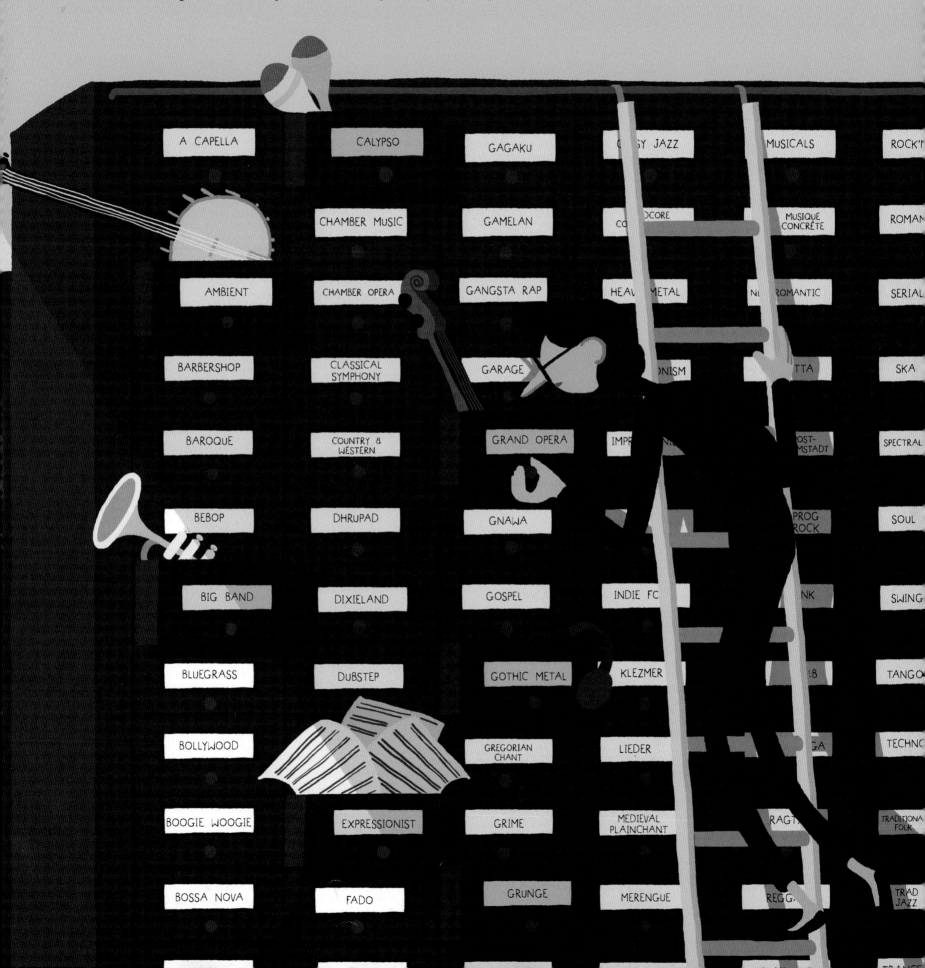

What is classical music?

COMPOSERS STARTED TO WRITE MUSIC DOWN AROUND ONE THOUSAND YEARS AGO...

Although the Great Basement of Musical Pigeonholes brings everything together into, well, one great basement, we should talk about some of the overarching categories of musical style and explain why these broader labels can be helpful.

As the Maestro, it falls to me to tell you about classical music. The term 'classical music' is a way of categorising the Western tradition of 'notated' music – music that is written down. This process of writing music down started in Europe as long as one thousand years ago, and we'll go into detail about how it works in Term 2.

Once you write music down, it becomes more fixed and formalised, but it also allows the composer to be really ambitious and demanding of the performers, because they

don't have to remember every note, and can practise the tricky bits in advance!

Some people might think that classical music comes from the past, that it is old-fashioned museum music, and that it has little or no relationship with the present. I think this is wrong twice over! First, classical music is being created right now, all around the world, by composers who are very much alive and kicking. And second, the act of performance brings music alive again – it becomes a living, breathing thing in the here and now, even if it was first written down hundreds of years ago.

Classical music is fantastically varied, and it has changed a lot over time. Many hundreds of years ago, in Medieval and Renaissance times, most music was written for the

Church, royalty and the nobility. Much of this music was religious, involving solo singers or choirs and only small numbers of instruments. In more recent times, composers have written for a wider public, for people paying money to attend concerts and operas, and to be entertained in buildings other than churches, cathedrals and royal palaces.

Generally speaking, classical music has got louder over the centuries! The Baroque-period orchestra that composers such as Vivaldi, Handel and J. S. Bach wrote for consisted usually only of string instruments, trumpets and a few woodwind instruments. There were perhaps only 15–20 of them, whereas by the time Haydn and Mozart were writing their symphonies (1760–1800), an orchestra's size had grown to 30–40, and

CLASSICAL · ROMANTIC · 1900 · MODERN

1820

... AND CLASSICAL MUSIC WAS BORN!

featured newly invented instruments such as the clarinet. The full-sized Romantic and Modern symphony orchestra, numbering 80–90, features larger numbers of all instruments, and ones that composers such as Mozart and Beethoven would not have known, such as the tuba and a wide range of percussion instruments.

It is hard to make sweeping statements about the different styles and periods of classical music, but whereas Baroque music is quite decorative and elaborate, the Classical period of Haydn and Mozart sounds to us more ordered and formal. Beethoven paved the way in the Romantic era for bigger sweeps of expression, drama and passion (the big names here are Wagner, Tchaikovsky and Rachmaninov). And in our ever-continuing

Modern period, composers have been bold, experimental and adventurous – breaking rules and making up new ones to create a wonderful range of new sounds and styles. Listen to composers such as Stravinsky, Messiaen, Shostakovich, Britten and Reich, and you will hear great, diverse riches.

As you listen to more and more classical music, stylistic differences will become ever clearer. You will be able to recognise the style and the period as distinctly as you might spot the difference between a grand, stone-carved cathedral and a shiny, steel-and-glass skyscraper. Classical music can be grand and intimate, just as an extravagant royal palace is a different place to live in than a cosy little cottage.

ACTIVITY

Listen to some classical music from different periods. How many instruments can you hear? Which words would you use to describe each piece – loud, quiet, fast, slow, grand, dramatic?

What is pop music?

So how did 'Pop Music' get its label? Well, the word 'pop' stems from 'popular'… But the problem with this term is that 'popular music' suggests that other kinds of music are un-popular, which definitely isn't right! Popular music is a kind of catch-all phrase for music of its day with wide appeal. Its most distinct characteristics, compared with other kinds of music, are the short song structures and a consistent – often driving – beat.

Pop music is generally thought to have come into being in the 1950s, when rock 'n' roll took off in the United States, with people like Buddy Holly and Elvis Presley plugging their guitars in and rocking the nation! Pop and rock bands developed from there, The Beatles being the first to achieve mass global popularity in the 1960s. Since then, pop and rock music has travelled the world over, reinventing itself each decade as bands embraced new technology, experimented with different sounds and forged new styles.

But if we think of 'pop' or 'popular' music as being something for 'the people', something with mass popularity, then it has existed for centuries! There have always been songs for the people – songs for storytelling and songs of love – and there has always been dance music.

Long ago, such music was passed down from one generation to the other by ear, by listening and remembering (it wasn't written down). We would now call 'folk music'. In the earlier part of the 20th century, before pop and rock carved out their own identities,

POP MUSIC
HAS CONSTANTLY
REINVENTED
ITSELF

dance music and popular songs became more closely linked to jazz, blues and swing. Today, folk music has developed as a separate musical branch, and it continues to reinvent itself in rich and wonderful ways.

When the term 'classical music' was first established in the mid-19th century, and until fairly recently, there was an assumption that it was the only music that would last for a long time, whereas other kinds of music that weren't written down (like folk and pop music) would be forgotten by future generations.

This all changed when recordings came along over a hundred years ago. All the different ways of capturing music performances – from old vinyl LPs to video and downloads – have given all kinds of music a chance to live into the future. Something that was improvised and created 'for the moment' has as much chance of a long life now as something written down and 'classical'. The best pop music has achieved classic (not to be confused with classical) status!

ACTIVITY

What are your favourite pop songs? Ask an older person to play you some pop or rock music from when they were younger. Does it sound different to the music you hear today?

What is jazz?

Mmmm! 'Jazz' is another word that's very hard to define. People recognise jazz when they hear it, but it's a genre of music that has existed for over a hundred years and has developed and changed around the world in that time… a lot!

Just like with classical music, if people say they like jazz – or if they say they don't like jazz – it's hard to really know what they mean. It's like someone saying, "I like the countryside". Is that flat or hilly countryside? Are there lots of trees, or lakes and rivers?

No-one knows for sure where the word 'jazz' came from, but it's likely that it was a slang American word in the 19th century meaning energy, spirit and courage. Jazz music (though no-one calls it 'jazz music', it's just 'jazz'!) started off in the southern states of the USA, in particular the city of New Orleans in Louisiana. It came together from a mix of musical styles: brass marching band, the blues and spirituals of African-Americans, the Cuban habanera dance, and ragtime – music whose rhythms were 'ragged' through going

off-beat (also known as 'syncopation' – see Lesson 20 for more on this).

As a percussionist, I play both classical and jazz, and they are equally challenging in their different ways. In jazz, improvisation is king! Improvisation is the freedom to make music up as you go along, to create something 'in the moment'. It means that no two performances of a jazz piece are the same. Jazz performers are brilliant listeners: they need to listen hard to what is happening around them, and react with split-second timing.

NO TWO PERFORMANCES OF A PIECE OF JAZZ ARE THE SAME

ACTIVITY

Improvisation is king in jazz! And it's not just instrumentalists that improvise. Singers do, too. This is called scat singing. Try it yourself: choose your own melody and make up the words, too. Doo-bop shewop!

Does music sound different around the world?

MANY MUSICAL CULTURES DEVELOPED IN ISOLATION FROM ONE ANOTHER, WHICH IS WHY THEY SOUND SO DIFFERENT

In our Great Basement of Musical Pigeonholes, we have lots of musical styles from around the world. But so far in our discussion of classical, jazz and pop, we haven't strayed very far from music originating in the Western world – yet.

So much wonderful music comes from other cultures and other continents. To 'Western ears' it sounds completely different: the instruments are different, the singing styles are different and the rhythms, melodies and harmonies are different, too! Much less music from non-Western cultures is written down, but it can be highly organised (like Western classical music). In fact, many cultures have centuries-old traditions of their own 'classical music'; just ask an Indian sitar-player or a Malian kora-player.

Many musical cultures developed in isolation from one another, which is why they sound so distinctive. In 1889, a big gathering of global cultures called the World Exhibition was held in Paris. This was one of the first times that Western musicians heard (what to them were) exotic sounds from other parts of the world, such as a Javanese gong orchestra, or gamelan. Composers such as Claude Debussy found this very influential on their style.

In the 20th century, some composers became fascinated by different countries' folk cultures, and they started writing down and recording folk songs. Once again, the boundaries of classical and non-classical traditions become mixed up!

ACTIVITY

Go online and try searching for music from different parts of the world. What does the music make you think of? Draw a picture based on the sounds you can hear.

More recently, different musical cultures from around the world have been brought together under a new label: 'world music'. All of this has opened our ears to a big, wide musical world. It has also led to styles of music from different cultures getting mixed up, which can be a good thing… and sometimes a bad thing! Mixing Italian lasagne with Indian curry might not taste great – it takes a skilled cook to mix the flavours well!

Which musical instruments do we hit?

As a percussionist, boy do I need to be able to count. As well as having ferociously difficult rhythms to cope with, I also have a lot of bars' rest in orchestral music, and woe betide if I forget to clash the cymbals or bang the drum at the right time!

Percussion is divided into two types: 'tuned percussion' and 'untuned percussion'. Tuned percussion, which produces identifiable pitches, includes instruments such as the xylophone, glockenspiel, marimba, vibraphone, tubular bells, crotales and timpani (kettle drums). And then there's the rest: snare drum, bass drum, rototom,

cymbals, triangle, tambourine, maracas, cowbell, castanets and my favourite, the wonderfully-named vibraslap.

When I play rock, pop or jazz, I play a drumkit. The conventional set-up consists of the bass drum, crash cymbal, floor tom, hi-hat cymbals, tom-tom and snare drums.

And then there are lots of other wonderful drums from around the world: the West African djembe, the tabla and double-headed dhol drum from India, the Iranian goblet drum the zarb and the Irish frame drum, the bodhran.

ACTIVITY

If you're going to be a drummer, you need to be able to do lots of different things with your hands and feet – all at the same time. Try patting your head with one hand and rubbing your stomach with the other hand at the same time.

BOY DOES A PERCUSSIONIST NEED TO BE ABLE TO COUNT!

Which musical instruments do we play with keys?

You might think of a piano, if someone asks you about instruments with keys. But there are all sorts of instruments with a set of keys that the player presses to produce notes, and in many cases, that keyboard is the only thing that these varied instruments have in common! Pianos and harpsichords have strings inside them... but the celeste doesn't – it has bells inside instead! And with an organ, the keys are connected to pipes. A piano accordion, with its squeezebox, is even in some ways a wind instrument!

The modern piano has hammers that strike a set of strings inside the body of the instrument – so Roxy might say that the piano is actually a percussion instrument.

The harpsichord looks like an older version of the piano, but in fact it doesn't have hammers, it has little devices that pluck the strings instead.

Other keyboard instruments are entirely electronic, such as the futuristic-sounding synthesizers that became popular from the 1960s onwards.

KEYBOARD INSTRUMENTS PRODUCE SOUND BY HITTING, PLUCKING, BLOWING... AND PLUGGING IN!

ACTIVITY

You need good muscles in your fingers to play a keyed instrument. Put each hand on a table, as though there were a small apple underneath, and balance a coin on top. Can you lift and wiggle each finger one by one, without the coin falling off?

Lesson 10

Which musical instruments are played with a bow?

KEMENCHE

REBEC

REBEC BOW

DOUBLE BASS

ERHU

ESRAJ

REBAB

Some of the oldest and loveliest musical instruments in the world are made out of bits of wood, gut and horsehair. That doesn't sound very nice, does it? Well, it's true! (Although the 'strings' that the horsehair 'bow' is drawn over are usually made of steel and nylon nowadays.)

Bowed string instruments come in all shapes and sizes. The best-known is the violin (also known as the 'fiddle', especially in folk music) and its bigger siblings are the viola, the cello and the double bass. The very best of these are extremely valuable and precious – they are worth a lot more than a big house! Some were made 350 years ago in Italy, and if looked after properly they just get better and better. The most famous violin and cello maker was Antonio Stradivari. Rufus has been lent a 'Strad' by some wealthy people and he is always nervous that it will get damaged or stolen.

The violin family's older cousins were instruments such as the lyra and rebec; they were popular more than a thousand years ago in Europe. The rebec's close relation, the rebab, is still widely played in North Africa and the Middle East, as is the kemenche in

THE STRINGS ARE THE LARGEST
SECTION OF THE ORCHESTRA

- STRINGS
- WOODWIND
- BRASS
- PERCUSSION

VIOLIN

ACTIVITY

Go online and listen to Vivaldi's *The Four Seasons*, Tchaikovsky's *Serenade for Strings* and Herrmann's film score for *Psycho*. Listen to how these different composers write for orchestral strings.

countries such as Turkey and Iran. In different parts of India, the esraj and dilruba are played. The erhu is the most common member of the Chinese huqin family of bowed instruments, and there are many more instruments elsewhere, too!

Strings are particularly important to me, the Maestro, because they are, if you like, the engine room of every orchestra. I have lots of string players in mine, and the leader of the orchestra – who is always a violin player – sits right under my nose as I conduct.

The violins are joined by viola players (such a mellow and mesmerising sound), cellists and double bassists – the biggest and deepest member of the string family. Remember: the bigger the instrument, the deeper the sound.

Lesson 11

Which musical instrument does everyone have?

And after describing all these instruments, from different countries and different cultures, the one instrument all human beings have in common is our singing voice. The voice box – officially, the larynx – is one of the human body's most amazing things. It's certainly mine!

There are many different styles of singing – folk, pop, jazz, classical, choral. I am an opera singer, which means I have trained all the muscles in my throat and chest to produce a certain kind of sound. It's pretty powerful, my friends… no microphone needed here!

The highest female voice is a soprano – I'm a soprano, and I can blast it out quite high! The lower-sounding female voices are (in order, high to low) the mezzo soprano and the contralto (often known as an 'alto').

The highest adult male voice is a tenor, although when a man sings in his 'falsetto' (the Italian for a false voice – faking it) he is known as a counter-tenor or male alto. Or a BeeGee! The lower male voices are baritone and bass. Basses go very, very low (especially when they've just woken up in the morning).

THE ONE INSTRUMENT PEOPLE ALL OVER THE WORLD HAVE IN COMMON IS THEIR VOICE

ACTIVITY

Try some of Diva's vocal warm-ups. Roll your rrrrs. Sing lots of short, sharp notes, "Ha, ha, haa!" Next, mimic a siren, "Woo-oo!". How high can you sing? How low can you go? How long can you hold one note?

Nowadays, any piece of music that you download tends to be called a 'song'. The problem with this is that not all pieces of music involve people singing. The accurate definition of a song is a piece of music that involves someone singing. The clue is in the name – a song is sung!

Most 'pop songs' – to gather all sorts of music into one super-huge category – involve someone singing. And most downloads are pop songs. So, technically, most people are downloading songs when they're downloading 'songs'. But at the School of Music, we like to keep our definitions tight. A song is a song if it's sung. La la! La la! So if your download is a piece of orchestral music or some African drumming, your download is NOT A SONG!

A SONG IS A SONG IF IT'S SUNG,

WITH YOUR MOUTH AND TEETH AND TONGUE.

IF <u>JUST</u> STRINGS OR HORNS REACH YOUR EAR,

THEN A SONG IS <u>NOT</u> THE THING THAT YOU HEAR.

IF <u>JUST</u> HARPS OR PIPES FILL THE AIR,

THEN A SONG IS <u>NOT</u> WHAT'S PLAYED OVER THERE.

A SONG IS A SONG IF IT'S SUNG,

WITH YOUR MOUTH AND TEETH AND TONGUE.

What happens when you bring different musicians together?

Making music with other people is great fun! A gathering of musicians is called a group, a band, an ensemble, an orchestra – or, if you're singing, a choir. It all depends on the style of music you're making. Over the years, some classic combinations have evolved: the string quartet, the jazz trio of piano, bass and drums, or the pop group foursome of guitar, bass, drums and vocals. Small ensembles of musicians in classical music evolved gradually into small orchestras about 400 years ago, but as Sergio mentioned in Lesson 2, they

grew and grew in the 18th and 19th centuries. The biggest symphony orchestras now contain up to a hundred musicians.

Pop and rock line-ups stick to no fixed pattern, though. The singer might play guitar too. There might be a keyboardist playing piano and synthesizers. And there may be other instruments in the mix too, like saxophones or brass.

When instruments play together, they each take on different roles. For instance, in the School of Music rock band Roxy plays the

drums and keeps the beat, while Rufus plays the bassline. Together, they are the rhythm section of the band – joined sometimes by Niagara or Ronny playing chords on the piano and guitar. Diva sings the melody, and if Ronny is playing a lead guitar, sometimes she will stop for long enough to give him time for a solo. (Not always though.) Different bands have different line-ups, but each player always has a particular role so that the music makes sense to the people listening.

IN A BAND, EACH PLAYER HAS A PARTICULAR ROLE

ACTIVITY

Build your own fantasy band. Who will you ask to join? Which instruments will you each play? Will you have a singer? What genre of music will you play? What costumes will you wear?

What is a string quartet?

A STRING QUARTET HAS
TWO VIOLINS, ONE VIOLA
AND ONE CELLO

One of classical music's most enduring combinations of instruments is the string quartet. This line-up, featuring two violins, one viola and one cello, has been a favourite of many composers for the last 250 years. When you see and hear a string quartet perform, it's like listening in on a fascinating conversation.

Early on, the first violin tended to be given most of the tunes, with the second violin and viola usually playing lower accompaniment figures and the cello providing the supporting bassline. Later on, all four instruments acquired a greater equality in their roles.

The first composer to recognise the string quartet's huge musical potential was Joseph Haydn. He liked the string quartet so much, he wrote nearly 70 pieces of music for them! That's about 30 hours of music.

Other composers who wrote lots of fantastic music for string quartet include Haydn's friend Wolfgang Amadeus Mozart (he only wrote 25 or so pieces of music – but he didn't live as long), Haydn's pupil Ludwig van Beethoven (he wrote a mere 16), and two other composers who lived in Vienna in the 19th century – Franz Schubert and Johannes Brahms. Haydn's brilliant musical invention has travelled far and wide since. Amazing string quartet music has been written all over the world, not least by the Russian composer Dmitri Shostakovich and the Hungarian Bela Bartok in the middle of the 20th century.

The string quartet has turned out to be pretty adaptable. You can hear it, for example, in The Beatles' song 'Eleanor Rigby' and Coldplay's 'Viva la Vida'.

How do music and the movies go together?

When you experience the hi-tech spectacle of a movie now, it's hard to imagine that when they first started making films well over a hundred years ago, the moving pictures were all you got – black-and-white ones, not colour either. There was no way, until the 1920s, of attaching sound to the pictures. Which is why those early films have become known as Silent Movies.

Except they weren't entirely silent! They used to have live musical accompaniment – often made up in the moment – by someone like Niagara playing a piano or organ in the cinema. That's how important music is! Even those first movies just couldn't do without it.

When technology caught up, the musical 'soundtrack' was pre-recorded and embedded into the film alongside all the dialogue from the actors. And that's when movie music really took off.

American entertainer Al Jolson started it all in 1928 with his all-singing, all-dancing performance in *The Jazz Singer*. And about ten years later, just before colour films went back to black-and-white during the Second World War (because they were too expensive to produce), four amazing films with four amazing soundtracks emerged: *Snow White and the Seven Dwarfs*, *The Wizard of Oz*, *Robin Hood* and *Gone with the Wind*.

The first two of these great films featured songs that became instant favourites: 'Heigh-Ho', 'Whistle While You Work', 'Some Day My Prince Will Come' and 'Somewhere Over the Rainbow'. If they're not favourites already, they will be once you've heard them...

The second two – scored by Erich Korngold and Max Steiner – set the standard for lush orchestral film-scores. Their gorgeous tunes and stirring, emotional climaxes made the film-bit of the films even better. Music does that. It enhances the action on screen. It makes the exciting bit even more exciting. It makes the scary bit even more scary. It makes the sad bit even sadder.

MUSIC MAKES THE EXCITING BITS EVEN MORE EXCITING!

THE SCHOOL OF MUSIC ASKS ITS TEAM ABOUT THEIR FAVOURITE FILM SCORES OF ALL TIME

There's some cool jazz in *The Aristocats*, and I'm a great fan of John Barry's James Bond scores. Double-oh heaven.

I love the sweeping epic music in *The Lord of the Rings*, by Howard Shore. He also composed the music for *The Hobbit*.

Bernard Herrmann is my hero. It doesn't get any more tense and thriller-enhancing than his *Psycho* soundtrack for Alfred Hitchcock.

When I was a young I played on a lot of John Williams's film score recordings. If you listen hard, you can hear me on *Jaws*, *E.T.*, *Star Wars* and *Indiana Jones*. They are all brilliant… and not just because of me!

I have to go for a musical, but which one? I've starred in so many! *West Side Story*, *Oliver!*, *Les Miserables*…? Rodgers and Hammerstein's music and lyrics in *The Sound of Music* are perfect, so maybe that.

Disney classics are some of my absolute favourites, such as *Snow White and the Seven Dwarfs*, *Mary Poppins* and *The Jungle Book*. Elton John and Hans Zimmer did a fantastic job with the recent classic *The Lion King*.

How do music and theatre go together?

Music is great to listen to, but it's even better when it's married with glamorous costumes, make-up and scenery... Let the multi-media magic of opera and musicals begin!

Music first got up on stage in the late 1500s. These pioneering 'operas' took place in Italy. They combined poetry, dance, music and costumes, and over the centuries, Italy has remained central to opera.

Opera isn't just about Italy, though. Just like my own globetrotting lifestyle as a superstar soprano, this wonderful, extravagant artform has travelled around the world with huge success since its beginnings 500 years ago. I get to play tragic heroines, gorgeous lovers, queens and sorceresses. And I sing my parts in all sorts of languages — I don't mind telling you that I'm quite the linguist now. I sing in German (in operas by Beethoven, Wagner and Strauss), English (Purcell and Britten), Russian (Tchaikovsky — who also wrote fabulous ballets), Czech (Janacek), French (Saint-Saëns, Bizet and Berlioz), and, of course, Italian (Handel, Mozart, Rossini, Verdi and Puccini).

Opera can be serious stuff — stories of love, death, war and revenge, full of dramatic, emotional impact. They can also be funny and more light-hearted. And about 150 years ago, a new opera-like category evolved called 'light opera' or 'operetta'. Composer Arthur Sullivan teamed up with the witty writer W.S. Gilbert to create a series of hugely popular, English-language operettas like *The Mikado* and *The Pirates of Penzance*. In Vienna, people like Johann Strauss and Franz Lehar wrote equally celebrated, German-language operettas. These usually featured spoken dialogue as well as music, and it was out of this wonderful mix of music and theatre that came the more recent descendant of opera: musicals.

Some of the greatest musicals include *Oklahoma*, *Carousel* and *The Sound of Music* by Rodgers and Hammerstein, Jerome Kern's *Showboat*, Lerner and Loewe's *My Fair Lady* and Bernstein and Sondheim's *West Side Story*. Recent musicals are equally popular: *Les Miserables*, *Matilda*, Andrew Lloyd Webber's *Cats*, *Evita* and *Phantom of the Opera* are all huge hits, too!

MUSICALS ARE THE YOUNGER COUSINS OF OPERA AND OPERETTA

ACTIVITY

Put on your own piece of musical theatre for your friends or family. Make up a story and think about the music you can play or songs you can sing to bring out the happy, sad or scary bits.

How do music and dance go together?

It isn't only the case that music goes with dance; it's music that makes people dance in the first place. Music sets the pulse and the feel of the dance. You can dance to silence, or to a soundtrack running in your head, if you want – but it's not really the same.

There are almost as many kinds of dance as there are kinds of music, and often the name of the music is also the name of the dance: as is the case with the waltz (Austria), disco (USA), tango (Argentina), salsa (Cuba) and bhangra (India) for example.

There are particular kinds of music for clog dances, barn dances, line dances, belly dances and tap dances, each with their own rhythms and atmospheres.

Just as with music, dance moves can be improvised – so you go where your body, and the music, takes you – or they can be formally fixed, rehearsed and repeatable. Think of the choreographer as dance's equivalent of the composer – they plan and rehearse the moves with the dancers.

Ballet is the most formal marriage of music and dance. It's also thought to be the most graceful and technically demanding form of dance. Ballet dancers have to train as hard as musicians as they aspire for perfection in their art. The French word 'ballet' comes from the old Latin word to dance, 'ballare', and the artform began in Italy (what didn't begin in Italy?) about 500 years ago. It then developed significantly as composers like Lully and Rameau wrote ballet music for the royal courts of 17th and 18th century France.

The most famous composer-choreographer partnership was between the Russian composer Pyotr Ilyich Tchaikovsky and the ballet-masters Marius Petipa and Lev Ivanov. Together, they were responsible for the ballet classics *Swan Lake*, *The Sleeping Beauty* and *The Nutcracker*. Not bad going!

BALLET IS THE MOST FORMAL MARRIAGE OF MUSIC AND DANCE

ACTIVITY

Go online and listen to some ballet music, like *The Nutcracker*. Next, listen to some tango music, like 'La Cumparsita'. Do they make you want to dance differently? Can you match your movements with the music?

How do music and architecture go together?

ACTIVITY

Try clapping your hands in different spaces and listening to the acoustics. First try it in your bedroom. Then go to the bathroom and compare the sound the clap makes there. Does it sound different? Is there an echo?

MUSIC SOUNDS DIFFERENT IN DIFFERENT BUILDINGS AND SPACES

Both of my parents were architects, so I've always been interested in buildings. And music has always had a special relationship with the buildings that it's performed in.

If you click your fingers or shout out loud in a big bathroom, it sounds different to in a small, carpet-filled bedroom. Sounds bounce off the hard surfaces of a bathroom in a much more resonant, boomy way than in a bedroom, where the carpet, bedding, curtains and pillows soak up the sound. There's no bounceback or 'reverberation' there.

In this way, we hear music differently in different buildings and spaces. In a huge cathedral or church building, with its stone and stained-glass and high vaulted ceilings, you can hear the music bouncing back at you for several seconds after it has stopped. This is called an 'acoustic', and it can be a beautiful experience for the audience (if the music was written for that kind of acoustic). But it can also make the music sound unclear and 'muddy', and the musicians often find it hard to hear each other clearly. 'Drier' acoustics are better for this, and for making recordings. That's why recording studios are often designed to have little or no acoustic bounce back.

In-between reverberant churches and dry recording studios, acoustically speaking, is a wonderful range of specially designed concert halls and opera theatres around the world.

They come in all sorts of shapes and sizes. Some have room for 300 to sit down in, and some have room for 3,000. Some are hundreds of years old, and some are brand new. Some look like royal palaces on the outside, and some look like spaceships. And the more recent, hi-tech buildings come with an adjustable acoustic, so that you can make it drier or boomier with acoustic 'drapes' and echo chambers. Generally speaking, pop, rock and jazz concerts – which use microphones and electronic amplification to boost the sound – benefit from a drier acoustic. And there's nothing drier than the absolutely-no-acoustic of an open air concert in a sports stadium. Rock on!

Lesson 18

How do music and maths go together?

There's a saying that "music and mathematics go together", and I certainly know a few brainboxes from my time at school who were really good at both. Mind you, I know a lot of other brilliant musicians (like me!) who don't get on with maths at all.

But at its very basic level, music is all about numbers, counting and patterns. We'll learn more about all this in Term 2, but whenever you make music, you have to count your 'beats in a bar' to be in time with the music, and you have to count up and down the notes of the scale.

Those notes of the scale, known as pitches, vibrate at a certain number of 'soundwaves' per second. So pitches have numbers attached to them in two ways – as a number in a scale (eight white notes in each 'octave' as well as five black notes, together making up twelve semitones), and also as 'hertz' frequencies per second. Every time you go up an octave, the hertz number doubles. The note A above 'middle C' on the piano is 440 hertz (vibrations per second): therefore, one octave above it doubles to 880 hertz. One octave lower and it halves to 220 hertz, and one lower again it halves again to 110 hertz... and so on! So, numbers and patterns are everywhere in music.

AT A VERY BASIC LEVEL, MUSIC IS ALL ABOUT NUMBERS, COUNTING AND PATTERNS

Composers over the centuries have made lots of connections between numbers and sound. They have experimented with patterns of notes that go backwards and upside down, twice as fast or half speed, or those which are symmetrical or mirrors of themselves. Johann Sebastian Bach was particularly fond of the number three (he was very religious, and three is an important number for Christians). So, for example, his Brandenburg Concerto Number Three is in three sections, and it features three groups of three instruments – violins, violas and cellos. Other composers have even written into music (through structure and proportion) the numbers of the Fibonacci Sequence, in which each number is the sum of the previous two numbers (e.g. 1, 2, 3, 5, 8, 13, 21, 34, 55 etc.) or prime numbers (which are numbers that are only divisible by themselves or one).

ACTIVITY

Look at the pattern of white and black notes on Ronny's piano and copy out your own piano onto some paper. After some practice, can you learn to write down the octave pattern perfectly, without looking?

What are the principal elements of musical language?

After Term 1, your ears are open-wide. You know about a world of different musical instruments, styles and cultures. And hopefully you have started listening to all this difference with the enthusiasm of someone setting out on an exciting new journey.

In Term 2, we will equip you with a musical toolbox so that you can begin to speak the language of music yourself. As a listener, you don't need to be able to speak that language at all. But if you want to perform it, or write it down as a composer so that others can perform it, knowing about these basic 'nuts and bolts' of music is really useful. Even then, it's not essential, however! A lot of fantastic performers over the centuries have never learnt to 'read music'. The music they have performed – from medieval dances to the latest pop songs – has been learnt with their fingers, their voices and their brains, bypassing any music written down on paper.

Historians and archaeologists have established that the first music was written down – not on paper but on tablets of stone – many thousands of years ago in Ancient Greece. The amazingly sophisticated and precise system of 'Western staff notation' we now have dates back about a thousand years, when religious chants in the early Christian church began to be written down in books, and distributed to monasteries around Europe. It was a clever way of ensuring that what a monk or nun sang in

England or Germany would be pretty close to how it sounded in Rome. It would be a few hundred years before the printing press was invented, let alone the ability to record sound. Making and listening to recordings is something we can take for granted now, but it's worth remembering that sound recording technology only became mainstream and commercially viable at the start of the 20th century – which in the long history of music is quite recent!

Rhythm, melody and harmony are to music what proteins, carbohydrates and fats are to food. They are the principal building blocks of all music, and you will be introduced to all of them in Term 2. You will also encounter other important, associated musical concepts such as pulse, pitch, scales and chords; note values and intervals; the time signature, the key signature and the stave.

Don't worry if all this seems scary and foreign to you! All words and ideas are new to us when we first encounter them, and in time they can become extremely familiar. We can learn the language of music to different levels, just like we can either have a basic knowledge of a foreign language (so that we can say some simple phrases on holiday) or we can be totally fluent after years and years of practice. Take it step by step, with us as your first guide, and you can choose what level to take it to.

Finally, in Term 2, we return from squiggles and dots on a page of music manuscript paper to words that describe music. In particular, these are the words that instruct a performer how to perform a particular piece. Should it be fast or slow? Should it be loud or soft? Should it be expressive, heavy or spiky? The main language for all these performance instructions has developed over hundreds of years as Italian. But they can be in any language the composer chooses – French, German, English, Japanese – and they can be pretty bizarre too. The wonderfully eccentric French composer Erik Satie always came up with something funny or mysterious for performers to ponder: one piano piece, he said, should sound "like a nightingale with toothache"!

How do we write music down?

Some people say they can 'read music', and others say that they can't. But there was a time – approaching about a thousand years ago – when no-one could say they could read music, because there was no music written down for them to read!

Music notation is the system used to show how the music we hear can be written down using symbols. There are various forms of music notation around the world, and as we

also know, there is a lot of music that doesn't get written down at all.

Lots of countries, however, use Western classical 'staff notation', and that is mostly what you will learn about in the coming lessons. This way of writing music was first developed by monks, who wanted to find a way to write down the chants they sang. Over time, it developed to give more and more information about how the music should be sung or played.

The other common form of music notation is called 'tablature' which, rather than indicating a pitch, shows instead where the notes can be found on an instrument with frets, such as a guitar and ukelele.

Tablature is a kind of code. Each line represents a different string, and each number represents a fret (ridge on the fretboard). The numbers on the lines tell you the position your finger should be in, and in which order.

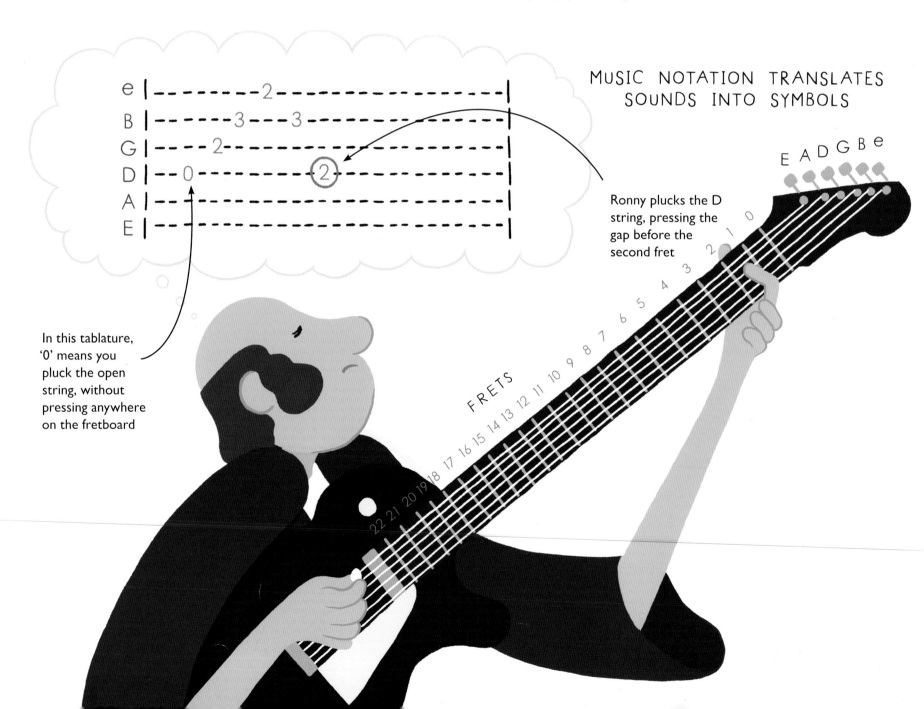

MUSIC NOTATION TRANSLATES
SOUNDS INTO SYMBOLS

Ronny plucks the D string, pressing the gap before the second fret

In this tablature, '0' means you pluck the open string, without pressing anywhere on the fretboard

ACTIVITY

Have fun creating your own graphic score. Anything goes – there's no right or wrong way to do this! Take a look at Roxy's example here and try to imagine what different sounds look like as marks on paper.

You can also have lots of fun with graphic scores. These are flexible representations of music using pictures and symbols instead of conventional musical notation. Think about the kinds of shapes that describe different sounds: for instance, my timpani (kettle drums) make deep, round sounds, my wood blocks make short, clicking sounds, whereas my triangle makes quick, sharp 'ting' noises! Graphic scores are also good for showing how the music should be played – quietly, energetically or gracefully.

What is rhythm?

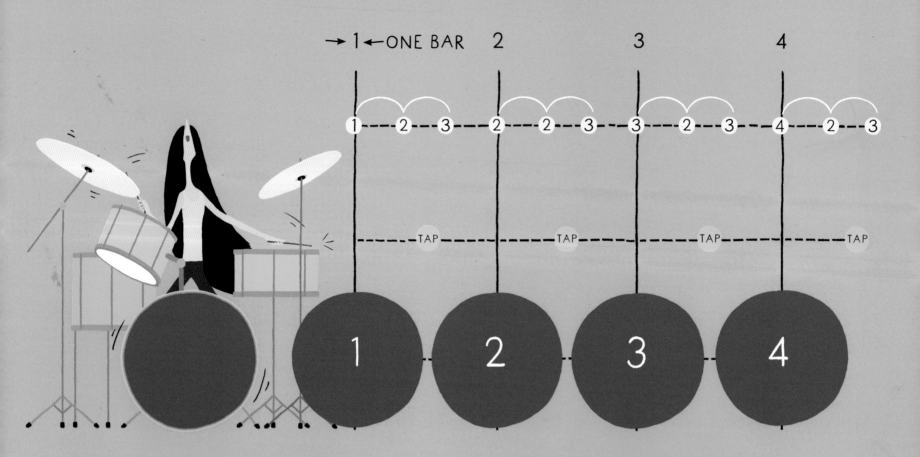

RHYTHM ARRANGES PATTERNS OF SOUND IN TIME

What would a piece of music sound like if every note were the same length? A bit boring! That is why rhythm is so important to musicians.

Rhythm arranges patterns of sound in time, and can be created using almost anything you can lay your hands on. Try clicking your fingers with a steady repetition (we call this a pulse), then clapping your hands, tapping your foot… you get the idea.

Let's see how it all works. First I'm going to produce a basic pulse with my foot on the kick drum like this: ONE, TWO, THREE, FOUR. If I repeat this pattern over and over again, I am creating separate 'bars' of four beats.

Next, I'll try an off-beat rhythm. I count to four out loud but tap the snare drum between the counts like this: (ONE) tap, (TWO) tap, (THREE) tap, (FOUR) tap. This is called syncopation.

Now I hit my cymbal in faster groups of three: ONE-two-three, ONE-two-three, ONE-two-three. These are known as triplets.

An effect called cross-rhythm is produced when two conflicting rhythms are heard together. This is tricky – get your concentrating head on and find a friend. Ask your friend to clap three beats: ONE-two-three, ONE-two-three, over and over, while you try to clap two beats: ONE-two, ONE-two, against the three. The ONE should always be together. It will take practice but it's fun when it works.

ACTIVITY

Try clapping out the three different rhythms Roxy describes here. First clap a steady pulse, ONE, TWO, THREE, FOUR. Then, try clapping on the off-beat, and sets of triplets. Good luck!

How do we write rhythm down?

DIFFERENT SYMBOLS REPRESENT DIFFERENT NOTE LENGTHS

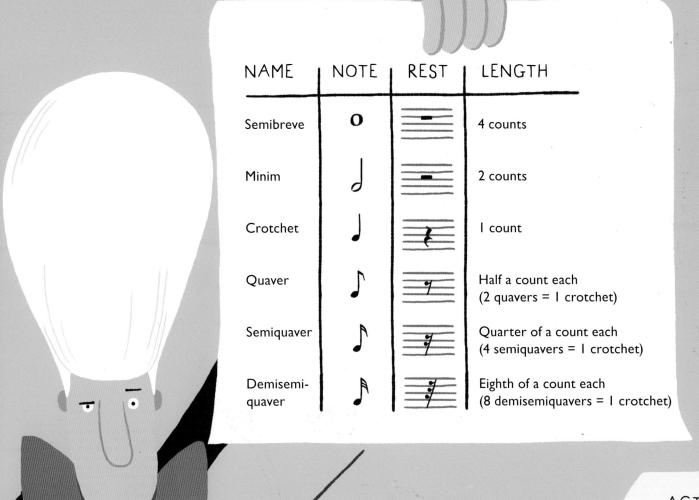

NAME	NOTE	REST	LENGTH
Semibreve	o	—	4 counts
Minim	𝅗𝅥	—	2 counts
Crotchet	♩	𝄽	1 count
Quaver	♪	𝄾	Half a count each (2 quavers = 1 crotchet)
Semiquaver	𝅘𝅥𝅯	𝄿	Quarter of a count each (4 semiquavers = 1 crotchet)
Demisemi-quaver	𝅘𝅥𝅰	𝅀	Eighth of a count each (8 demisemiquavers = 1 crotchet)

In Western notation, we write rhythm down with symbols that represent different note lengths. You can see here what the most common ones look like.

There are also times in music when you need to be quiet. We measure this silent time with rests – funny looking squiggles that sit on the stave and match up to note lengths, telling you not to play.

ACTIVITY

If a piece of music has four beats in each bar, how many different combinations of note lengths can you come up with? For example, one minim and two crotchets add up to four beats.

What is a time signature?

At the start of every piece of music using Western notation, you will find a time signature. This useful tool tells the performer how many beats will be contained in each bar. The time signature looks a bit like a fraction: $\frac{2}{4}$ or $\frac{3}{4}$ or $\frac{4}{4}$. The top number tells you how many beats you must count in each bar and the bottom number, what sort of beats we are using. So, the number 4 here at the bottom tells us we are counting in 'crotchets' and the top number, how many crotchets will be in each bar. So, $\frac{2}{4}$ would have two crotchet beats in each bar, $\frac{3}{4}$ would have three, and $\frac{4}{4}$ would have four. Most pop songs are in $\frac{4}{4}$ time and one of the best known types of music in $\frac{3}{4}$ time is the Viennese waltz, which Rufus and Diva are always happy to demonstrate.

But what happens if we see a piece of music in $\frac{5}{4}$ or $\frac{7}{4}$? Three well-known pieces that are in $\frac{5}{4}$ are the *Mission Impossible* theme tune, Dave Brubeck's 'Take Five' and 'Mars' from Gustav Holst's *The Planets*. And 'Money' from Pink Floyd's *Dark Side of the Moon* is in $\frac{7}{4}$. Have a listen to these and count out loud in five and seven.

THE TIME SIGNATURE TELLS YOU HOW MANY BEATS ARE IN EACH BAR

A WALTZ IS IN $\frac{3}{4}$

THREE BEATS IN A BAR

3
4

COUNTING IN CROTCHETS

ONE, two, three.

ONE, two, three.

Next we have $\frac{6}{8}$, $\frac{9}{8}$ and $\frac{12}{8}$: a new number at the bottom. This time we are counting in quavers – six, nine or twelve in a bar – and these time signatures often give music a springy, lively feeling. Ronny is dancing a jig, a dance particularly associated with $\frac{6}{8}$ time. Can you see how the notes are grouped in threes below? In these time signatures, each group of three quavers is thought of as being one count. So, $\frac{6}{8}$ time is counted as two beats in a bar, $\frac{9}{8}$ three beats in a bar and $\frac{12}{8}$ four beats in a bar.

So, as long as your bar of music contains the specified number of beats or counts, you can add all sorts of different note length combinations to bring your music to life. In a piece of music in $\frac{4}{4}$ for instance, you could have a bar with one semibreve, followed by a bar of two minims and then a bar of four crotchets. In $\frac{6}{8}$ you could write six quavers in bar one, followed by two dotted crotchets in bar two (a dot after a note value adds half as much duration again; dotted crotchets then are worth one and a half crotchets, or three quavers).

A JIG IS IN $\frac{6}{8}$

ACTIVITY

Count to four as you march around the room, stamping harder on ONE. Now, waltz around the room, counting to three, with the emphasis again on ONE. Which of these involves a different foot on the ONE beat?

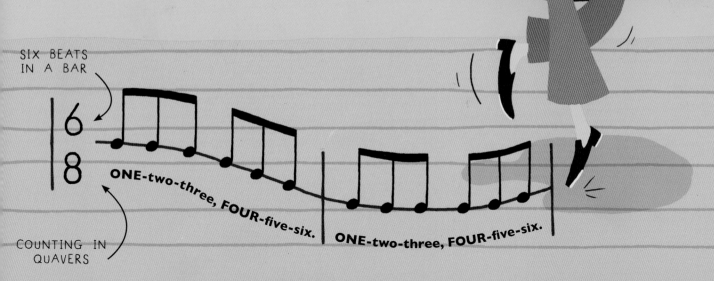

SIX BEATS IN A BAR

COUNTING IN QUAVERS

ONE-two-three, FOUR-five-six.   ONE-two-three, FOUR-five-six.

What is a stave and what is a clef?

The two main clefs used in Western notation are the treble clef and the bass clef. Some others that you may come across (depending on your instrument) are the alto and tenor clefs. Look below to see what they look like.

And what are those five lines that they are sitting on? That is the stave, or staff. Different notes are indicated by being placed over a line or in the spaces between the lines. Check out Lesson 24 for more on this!

Diva Venus favours the treble clef – the highest one – when she sings, whilst Rufus Vibrato is all about the lowest, the bass (with a dash of tenor now and again). The second highest, the alto clef, is Niagara's choice when she plays viola in the School of Music string quartet, and being a composer, Ronny is familiar with them all, including the second-lowest, the tenor clef.

RUFUS HAS THE LOW BASS CLEF.
FOR BASS, IT'S WHAT HE NEEDS,
NIAGARA PLAYS VIOLA –
IT'S THE ALTO THAT SHE READS.
I READ FROM THE TREBLE CLEF,
MY VOICE SOUNDS HIGH AND BRIGHT.
AND RONNY WRITES WITH ALL THE CLEFS,
(QUITE LATE INTO THE NIGHT!)

ACTIVITY

Copy out the five lines of the stave. Now practise the swirly treble clef. Do the same for the bass clef until you can do them without looking. Finally, try the other clefs.

BASS CLEF   TENOR CLEF   ALTO CLEF   TREBLE CLEF

What is a note?

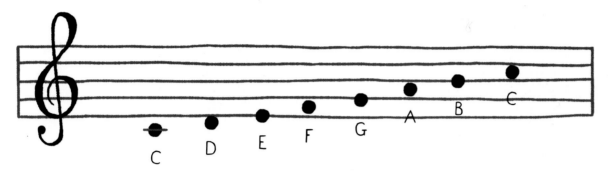

C D E F G A B C

EACH NOTE TELLS YOU THE EXACT PITCH YOU NEED TO SING OR PLAY

A FLAT SIGN LOWERS THE NOTE A SEMITONE

A SHARP RAISES THE NOTE A SEMITONE

A NATURAL SIGN CANCELS ANY FLATS OR SHARPS

Here again is our stave, but this time with blobs on! These blobs are called notes and where we put the blob gives it its note name. The note name tells you the exact pitch (how high or low) you need to sing or play.

The great thing is that you only need to know the first seven letters of the alphabet – once you've been through A, B, C, D, E, F and G, you start all over again with A!

If the notes are arranged in the order you see above, we have created a 'scale' – in this instance, the scale of C major, which only uses the piano keyboard's white notes. If we wanted to play or sing a scale starting on a different note, in order for it to sound the same as the scale of C, we would have to introduce some little symbols to ensure the notes sound the same. If the flat symbol is placed before a note, you would need to play that note a semitone lower. If you see a flat before the note B, for instance, you would play a B flat (on a keyboard, that is the black note in between B and A). The sharp sign raises the pitch by a semitone. A sharp sign placed before an F would raise the note from F to F sharp – this is also a black note nestled between F and G. (See Lesson 26 for more on intervals, tones and semitones.) The natural sign cancels out the sharps and flats completely.

What is a key signature and what effect does it have on music?

Most pieces of music are written in a key and therefore have a key signature. This sits on the stave, after the clef and before the time signature. Key signatures are made up of sharps and flats, and knowing which ones live in which key takes quite some time to learn! The key of F major has one flat, the key of D major has two sharps, and so on.

Major and minor keys can be responsible (alongside dynamics) for setting the mood of a piece of music.

Music written in a major key tends to sound upbeat and happy, whereas minor key music can sound sad, scary or mysterious.

Each key has its home note, C or D or E for example, and the key signature tells you which notes of the scale need sharpening or flattening. Every major key has a sister minor key with the same key signature, except in the minor keys, the third note is flattened, creating that sadder feel to the music.

ACTIVITY

Go online and search for Rachmaninov: Piano Concerto No.2 in C minor. Does it sound sad or happy to you? What does it make you think about?

IF YOU WATCH THE SAD OR SCARY MOMENTS IN A FILM LIKE 'HARRY POTTER', THE CHANCES ARE THE MUSIC IS IN A MINOR KEY

What is an interval?

The difference in pitch between two musical notes is called an interval. The smallest keyboard interval is called a semitone, or half a tone, and this is the distance on a keyboard between, for example, a C and a C sharp (or

D flat). A whole tone is made up of two semitones, so Sergio is jumping from F to G and ignoring the black note, F sharp. But of course, if Sergio had longer legs, he would be able to create much bigger intervals.

The distance between two notes is often bigger than just a semitone or a tone and we count these as thirds, fourths, fifths… and beyond. We measure these intervals by counting the distance between the two notes.

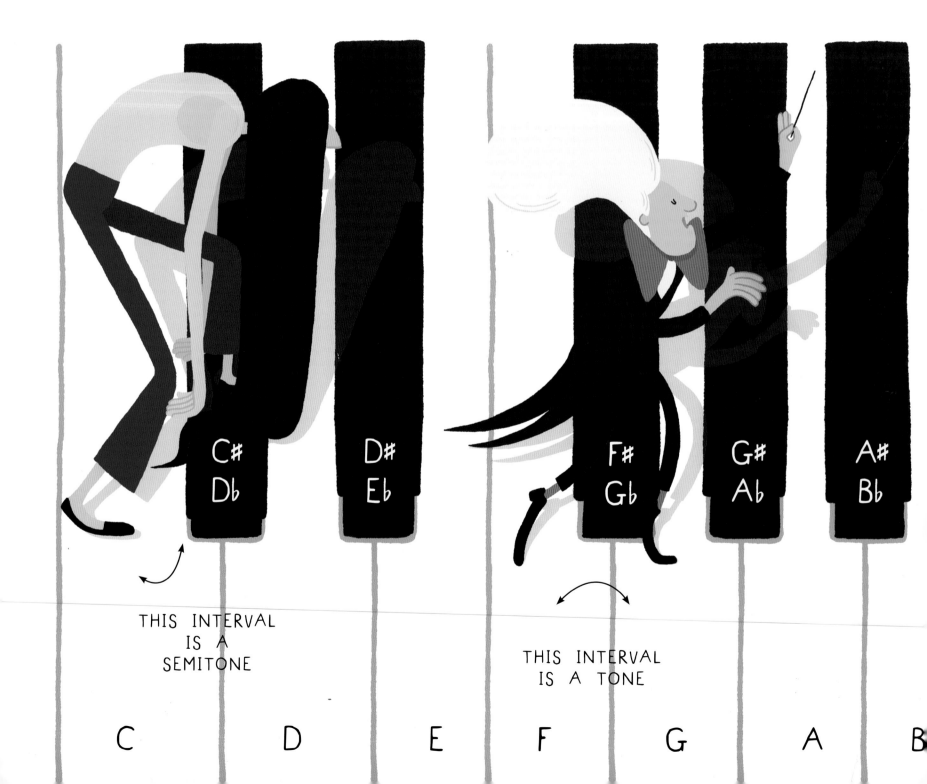

THIS INTERVAL
IS A
SEMITONE

THIS INTERVAL
IS A TONE

C   D   E   F   G   A   B

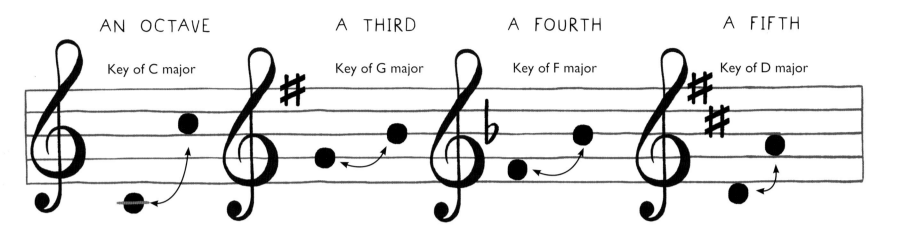

AN OCTAVE   A THIRD   A FOURTH   A FIFTH

Key of C major   Key of G major   Key of F major   Key of D major

AN INTERVAL IS THE DIFFERENCE IN PITCH
BETWEEN TWO NOTES

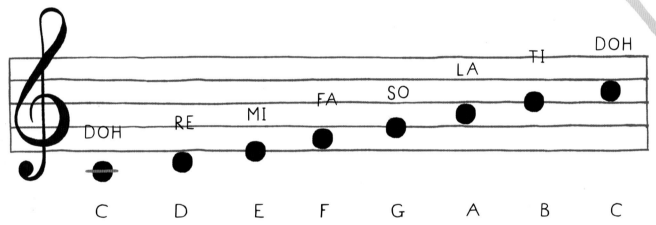

DOH   RE   MI   FA   SO   LA   TI   DOH

C   D   E   F   G   A   B   C

If you think back to Lesson 18, you might remember that the distance between one C and the next C is called an octave – representing the eight notes of a common scale. So, by looking at our keyboard, we would be able to work out that the distance from C to E is called a third, from C to F a fourth, and from C to G a fifth. I wonder what we would call an interval from C to A? And then C to B?

Aside from the usual major and minor scales, there are other ways of scaling an octave. For instance, you can make five whole tone jumps from C to C (C D E F# G# A# C). This is called the whole-tone or pentatonic scale.

ACTIVITY

Look at the scale above. The interval between C and G is a fifth. Starting with C, count all the notes on the way up to G – how many are there? Does it match the interval?

What is melody?

When you join together a series of different pitches, using a variety of intervals, you create a melody. Otherwise known as a tune! As an example, let's think of our 'Happy Birthday' tune again. It is made up of four musical sentences, or phrases. The first and second have identical rhythms, and are very similar in melodic contour, except that the first phrase contains the interval of a fourth, and in the second a fifth. The third phrase involves a big octave leap, and the fourth a sequence of smaller intervals.

A melody can be anything you want it to be – there are so many different notes to choose from, and so many different rhythmic combinations available. The possibilities are limitless!

CHOOSE A CLEF FROM THE SHELF.

ACTIVITY

Create your own melody. Draw a stave, add a clef and choose a key signature (C major is the easiest – no sharps or flats!). Then, decide on the time signature, and next add the notes and rests.

TRY USING NOTES AND RESTS OF DIFFERENT LENGTH, AND DON'T FORGET TO MAKE SURE EACH BAR ADDS UP TO YOUR TIME SIGNATURE

REMEMBER TO GIVE
YOUR MELODY SHAPE
AND STRUCTURE

HERE'S THE TIME SIGNATURE SHELF

NEED A KEY SIGNATURE?
SHARPS AND FLATS ARE HERE

DON'T FORGET YOUR BAR LINES

WELCOME TO MY COMPOSITION WORKSHOP!
COPY MY STAVE AND GET COMPOSING!

What is harmony?

The melody line is all well and good, but you might want more than one note sung or played at a time!

In the School of Music choir, some of our students sing the melody line. Others add a different, usually lower line, and by doing that, the choir is singing 'in harmony'. This is much more interesting for people to listen to.

A sung melody is often accompanied, maybe on a piano or on a guitar, by chords. Chords are created when three or more notes are played or sung together. If they sound as if they fit perfectly, they are known as 'concordant' but if there is a clash, if something sounds a bit wrong, the chords are described as 'dissonant' or 'discordant'.

If you have access to a piano, try playing the chord of C. Find middle C and play E (two white notes up) and G (two more white notes up). This should sound very satisfying. Now, choose a completely random selection of notes and play them together. What does that sound like, I wonder?

The first chords you might learn are those called I, IV and V (or 1, 4 and 5). These root chords are commonly used in pop music and originate from twelve-bar blues. But these three chords are just the beginning of a wonderful adventure of music making. Music can be a lot more interesting and expressive when there is a greater range of harmony to underpin the melody.

THREE NOTES SUNG
TOGETHER FORM A CHORD

ACTIVITY

Chords are sometimes written with Roman numerals like this. Try copying them down and learning them:

1 = I	5 = V
2 = II	6 = VI
3 = III	7 = VII
4 = IV	8 = VIII

THIS IS HOW WE WORK OUT THE CHORDS FOR C MAJOR

CHORD 1 IS MADE UP OF THE FIRST, THE THIRD AND THE FIFTH NOTES OF THE SCALE, C E G.

CHORD 4 IS MADE UP OF THE FOURTH, SIXTH AND EIGHTH NOTES OF THE SCALE, F A C.

CHORD 5 IS MADE UP OF THE FIFTH, SEVENTH AND NINTH NOTES OF OUR SCALE, G B D.

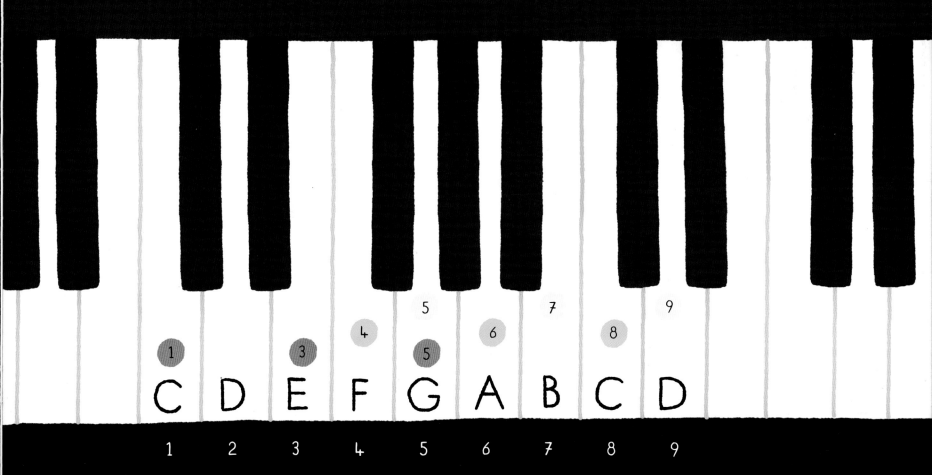

Lesson 30

How does a performer know how to play the music?

TEMPO IS THE SPEED AT WHICH A PIECE SHOULD BE PLAYED

ADAGIO
(QUITE SLOW)

LENTO (SLOW)

ANDANTE (WALKING PACE)

When Niagara or I write a piece of music, we imagine it being played in a certain way. For instance, if I have written a fanfare for an opening ceremony, I want it to be played fast and loud to sound impressive! And if I am writing music for a sad film, I want it to be played sensitively and slowly. But how can I give this information to the performer if I'm not there when they play it?

That's where performance directions come in! These are words or symbols on the page that give the performer this crucial, extra information. It's really useful stuff. And an extra bonus is that, unless you already speak Italian, you get to learn some words in a different language too, because most performance directions are in… Italian!

Going back several hundred years, so many important composers were Italian – or worked in Italy – that Italian became the main musical language. Many important musical words, such as 'concerto', 'opera', 'aria', 'cadenza', 'sonata' and 'tempo' are all Italian, and so are the words that composers use to give other performance directions. I add a tempo indication to every piece I write – this tells the musicians the speed at which the piece should be played. Each speed has a different word – in Italian of course!

ACTIVITY

Learn a little Italian! Write down each of the tempo directions here on small pieces of paper, and try to remember what they mean. Can you arrange them in order from slowest (lento) to the fastest (prestissimo)?

ALLEGRO
(QUITE FAST)

PRESTO
(FAST)

PRESTISSIMO
(VERY FAST)

Piano	*p*	Quietly
Mezzo piano	*mp*	Moderately quietly
Mezzo forte	*mf*	Moderately loudly
Forte	*f*	Loudly
Fortissimo	*ff*	Very loudly
Fortepiano	*fp*	Loudly, then quietly
Sforzando	*sfz*	Suddenly accented
Crescendo	<	Getting louder
Diminuendo	>	Getting quieter

ANIMATO
(ANIMATED)

DYNAMICS TELL THE
PERFORMER HOW
LOUDLY TO PLAY

When Niagara or I compose, tempo isn't the only thing we want to be able to tell performers about. We also give directions called dynamics, to say how noisily to play. We use Italian words to tell the performer to play loudly – 'forte!' – or quietly – 'piano'. If we want to add drama to a piece of music, we might ask them to start quietly and get louder and louder – this is called a 'crescendo'. Or, to make the music fade away and get quieter, we write 'diminuendo'.

We sometimes add some directions to tell the performer the style to play in right at the beginning of the piece, before they've got started. For instance, if we want the music to sound playful, we write 'scherzando', or if we want it to sound heavy, we write 'pesante'. We can also give directions on how the performer should play their instrument. If we want string players to pluck instead of bow, we write 'pizzicato', and if we want a clarinet to play short, sharp notes, we write 'staccato'. Basically, we can get whatever we want… if we write it in Italian!

How can we make music at home?

You might think that making music at home is impossible if you don't have any instruments to play. Think again! Being a percussionist, I head straight to the kitchen when I feel like setting up my own orchestra. It's the best place to look for interesting sounds.

The first thing I pull out of the cupboards (with permission, of course) are all the saucepans! Remember the rule – the bigger the instrument, the lower the sound. Find a wooden spoon and have a go. And lids! Oh my, they sound like big cymbals in an orchestra when bashed together. Knives and forks and spoons make a fantastic sound if they're popped into a carrier bag and shaken gently, or tapped together. Spoons can even be used to make exciting sounds like Spanish castanets. Take a look online if you don't believe me!

Next, look in the food cupboard. Grab a tube of crisps. Pour out the crisps and fill the empty tube with either dried rice or dried pasta, like Ronny. Give them a shake.

If you really want to go to town, ask a grown-up to come and help. Put eight glasses in a row (thinner glasses have the nicest 'ting'!). Fill each glass with a different amount of water from just a little to almost full, just like Niagara. Take a small spoon and ever-so-gently tap the glass to see if the sounds are different. Alter the amount of water in each to 'tune' the glasses into a scale. Then, make up a melody by tapping the glasses.

Are there any little stubby glass bottles hanging around in the recycling? Give them a wash and try playing them like a flute. Form a nice smile and gently blow over the top of the bottle. This takes time and practice! You can experiment with these in the same way as the glasses. Fill the bottle with water and see what that does to the pitch.

Take a look around – does anything else inspire you? What does an electric whisk sound like when it's on? Can you make a sound with the dustbin lid, or dustpan and brush?

Finally, grab a chopstick or drinking straw and use it like a baton (a conductor's stick) to bring your kitchen orchestra to attention. And off you go. How many different sounds can you get from your instruments?

THE KITCHEN IS THE BEST PLACE TO LOOK
FOR INTERESTING, PERCUSSIVE SOUNDS

ACTIVITY

Try making your own kitchen orchestra at home – asking permission first, of course! Experiment with the sounds by playing different 'instruments' together. What are your favourite combinations?

Why should we sing?
And when can we do it?

We all know someone who never stops singing or humming. Is that person happy? The chances are, yes! Because we now know that singing releases chemicals into our bodies that make us feel good. It certainly works for me!

The best thing about singing is that it is completely free. At the School of Music we are all big fans of singing in a choir, but you don't even have to leave your house to set up your own singing group. Who's around? Get your friends over and sing your favourite songs. Can one of you sing the tune and another add a harmony line? Remember to listen to each other – this is a big part of singing as a group.

Car journeys are the perfect time to get some singing going. One of my favourite games is to listen to the radio and, when you hear a song you know, sing along and try turning it down for a bit to see if you can keep in absolute time when the volume is turned back up. Take it in turns. Who is the best at it? I always win in our car!

Of course, you may have your sights set on a solo career like mine. If that is the case, little vocal exercises each morning will help to keep your vocal apparatus in shape. I begin by singing scales up and down to the vowel sounds, 'a, e, i, o, u'. Next, I work on my breathing. I slowly sip in a lungful of air, (making sure my shoulders don't rise up) and then I hiss the air back out. How long can you keep hissing for? And then, I let rip! I work on my singing every day, which is probably why I'm so very good.

SINGING RELEASES CHEMICALS INTO OUR
BODIES THAT MAKE US FEEL GOOD

ACTIVITY

Early in the morning,
open the window and listen
to the birds singing their
dawn chorus. Can you make
out any of the individual
songs? Try copying them and
singing them back into the
air, 'tra-la-la!' It's like having
a musical conversation
with nature!

How can we combat nerves?

I think any musician or performer – even a world-famous singer like myself – knows what stage fright feels like. That moment before you go on stage to perform in front of an audience (however small) can be terrifying. At my worse moments, my hands and knees shake, I feel hot and sweaty and my head starts to swim…

Learning how to overcome your nerves in order to play before a crowd is all part of your journey towards becoming a musician.

The good news is that over time, most musicians get more and more used to playing in front of others. You might even find that you start to look forward to it! But if, like me, you feel the nerves creeping up on you, you can try one of these techniques to help stay calm.

Be prepared. Know what you're performing inside out, tnorf-ot-kcab and upside down.

Most importantly, if you forget where you are, or have a memory slip, make it up! No one will even know…

Eat bananas! They'll give you lots of energy to keep focused and alert in your solo spot.

Make friends with the little butterflies floating around your tummy. They're producing the adrenalin needed to produce a fine performance.

IF YOU FEEL NERVOUS, TRY ONE
OF THESE TECHNIQUES TO HELP STAY CALM

Do a few star
jumps before you go
on stage to get the blood
coursing through your veins.

ACTIVITY

Practise how to walk
on to a stage and
perfect the art of looking
confident, even if
everything else goes
wrong! Try out your
bow, bending from the
waist with your hands
by your sides!

Think positive thoughts:
"I am simply wonderful."

How can we memorise music?

When you're used to playing with the music written down in front of you, it can be a bit daunting when you're asked to remember a piece and play it just relying on your memory.

I have developed a useful technique to help with this: chunking. Chunking is the way forward! I divide the piece of music up as though it were a chocolate bar, and I learn small sections, chunk by chunk. (Then, I like to reward myself by eating a chunk of chocolate. Nom, nom, nom.)

I practise each chunk slowly, first, playing *with* the music in front of me, then *without*, covering it up and repeating. Try using sticky notes to cover up every other bar, then swap the sticky notes over to reveal the previously hidden bars. Being a grown-up, it can take me a bit longer to learn by heart than my younger students at the School of Music, but it always works eventually.

To help jog my memory, I look for other things to help me remember a phrase or section. I also check out the performance directions and any other dynamic markings.

The thing that trips me up the most is concentration. If I forget where I am in a piece of music, it's usually because I've stopped concentrating. So before I start, I find my 'zone' – and stick with it until I reach the end!

DIVIDE THE PIECE OF MUSIC UP AS THOUGH IT WERE
A CHOCOLATE BAR, AND LEARN SMALL SECTIONS,
CHUNK BY CHUNK

ACTIVITY

Practise one bar over
and over until you have
it in your muscle
memory (so that your
fingers remember how
to play it without
reading the notes). Then
take away the music!
Can you still play it?

How do we look the part when we perform?

Playing or singing the right notes in the right place is very important in a performance – but that shouldn't be all that you aspire to. For your performance to be truly dazzling and memorable, you need to look the part, too. In very simple terms, this is about great body language. You need to walk on to the stage confidently. You need to engage the audience with sparkling eyes and a lovely smile… especially when you're graciously soaking up their applause! Always give the impression that you're in control, and that you're enjoying the experience. That way, your audience will enjoy it too.

Of course, the clothes you wear will affect the way you come across. People listen to music with their eyes as well as their ears. Different kinds of music have their own 'look', and the look of music has changed enormously over the years. Maybe because I don't have a lot of hair myself, I'm especially interested in the way musical hairstyles have changed over the centuries. Wigs can say a lot about how music sounds – so here's my little history of music in hair…

In medieval times, they started up a special hairstyle in monasteries by shaving the crown of each monk's head in a neat circle. The hairstyle never really caught on (frankly I'm not surprised – it's not a good look, is it?). But the religious music those monks chanted in their daily worship has been popular ever since.

Antonio Vivaldi, one of the Baroque era's greatest composers, was known as 'The Red Priest' because of the colour of his hair – a fiery red. But you'd never know it from the long, flowing white wig he always wore. Venice, where Vivaldi lived, gets pretty hot in the summer – and it must have been even hotter under that rug.

Right through the 18th century, composers such as Handel, Bach, Mozart and Haydn wore tidy, tightly-curled wigs. But in the early 19th century, Ludwig van Beethoven said a big 'No!' to fake hair and showed off what God gave him on top instead. His hair was as distinctive and convention-busting as his music was. Nowadays, people use lots of styling gel and mousse to get it looking like that. Ludwig just didn't wash it for months on end.

In the late 1960s, lots of young people grew their hair long. Though it was mainly a

PEOPLE LISTEN TO MUSIC WITH THEIR EYES AS WELL AS THEIR EARS –
DIFFERENT KINDS OF MUSIC HAVE THEIR OWN 'LOOK'

very hairy gesture of protest, these people known as hippies also saved a lot of money on haircuts. Musicians led the way, and as rock music got louder and more grandiose in the 1970s, so too did the hairstyles of their lead singers and guitarists. Some of those rockers, now ageing grandparents, still have impressively big hair.

Halfway through the 1970s, some slightly younger young people decided they really hated the music that the slightly older young people were making. Progressive Rock and Glam Rock definitely had to go – it was too musically ambitious, and the songs were getting even longer than the hair. Punk Rock was born: a music that was anti-music, anti-everything, deliberately offensive and unmelodious. Hairstyles changed almost overnight. Droopy, lank long hair became spiky, colourful and gravity-defying. For a few years, punks became a tourist attraction in London. The music was briefly influential, too.

From what I see with my students at the School of Music, hair is no less important today! There was a short time when 'Bieber Fever' ran riot in my classes and the mop-top was the must-have look.

But if none of these looks is your thing, then I urge you to experiment. Music is all about creativity – inside, and out!

ACTIVITY

Choose your outfit to perform in. What kind of clothes match the music you will be playing? Will you wear something very formal, or put on some kind of costume or disguise?

Books to inspire you further

GENEVIEVE HELSBY, JASON CHAPMAN

My First Classical Music Book (Naxos Books 2008)
Learn about composers and instruments of the orchestra in this book with lots of illustrations and an accompanying CD.

STEVEN ISSERLIS

Why Beethoven Threw The Stew (Faber & Faber 2001)
Why Handel Waggled His Wig (Faber & Faber 2006)
These two books by one of the world's greatest cellists give amusing biographical portraits of several major composers, such as Bach, Handel, Haydn, Mozart, Beethoven, Brahms and Tchaikovsky.

JAMES MAYHEW

Ella Bella Ballerina books (Orchard Books 2006)
These beautiful books are the perfect introduction for younger readers to ballets such as *Swan Lake*, *The Sleeping Beauty*, *The Nutcracker* and *Cinderella*.

VARIOUS

The Children's Book of Music (DK 2010)
This is another lavishly illustrated book with a CD, but this time covering all kinds of music.

VARIOUS

There are also lots of great tutorial books on the 'theory of music' which develop, stage by stage, your confidence with the nuts and bolts of music that we cover here in Term 2.

Films to inspire you further

AMADEUS

(Milos Forman 1984)
It's hard to imagine a more brilliant or engaging film about Mozart. The performances, the locations, the costumes and the screenplay all complement the perfection of Mozart's music.

FANTASIA

(Disney 1940)
Genius animation combined with great music and cartoon storytelling.

LATCHO DROM

(Tony Gatlif 1993)
Meaning 'Safe Journey' in the Roma language, this is a staggeringly beautiful portrait of gypsy music, featuring musicians and dancers from Rajasthan in India, Egypt, Bulgaria, Romania, France and finishing with Spanish flamenco.

Composers to inspire you further

This list could be two pages long! So here is just a relatively small selection to get you started.

MEDIEVAL

Hildegard von Bingen (1098–1179)
Pérotin (1160–1230)
Guillaume de Machaut (1300–1377)

RENAISSANCE

Josquin des Prez (c. 1450–1521)
Thomas Tallis (c. 1505–1585)
Giovanni Pierluigi da Palestrina (c. 1525–1594)
William Byrd (1543–1623)
Tomás Luis de Victoria (1548–1611)

BAROQUE

Claudio Monteverdi (1567–1643)
Henry Purcell (1659–1695)
Jean-Philippe Rameau (1683–1764)
George Frideric Handel (1685–1759)
Johann Sebastian Bach (1685–1750)
Antonio Vivaldi (1678–1741)

CLASSICAL

Joseph Haydn (1732–1809)
Wolfgang Amadeus Mozart (1756–1791)
Ludwig van Beethoven (1770–1827)

EARLY ROMANTICS

Gioachino Rossini (1792–1868)
Franz Schubert (1797–1828)
Hector Berlioz (1803–1869)
Felix Mendelssohn (1809–1847)
Frédéric Chopin (1810–1849)
Robert Schumann (1810–1856)
Franz Liszt (1811–1886)

LATER ROMANTICS

Giuseppe Verdi (1813–1901)
Richard Wagner (1813–1883)
Johannes Brahms (1833–1897)
Pyotr Ilyich Tchaikovsky (1840–1893)
Antonín Dvořák (1841–1904)
Edward Elgar (1857–1934)
Giacomo Puccini (1858–1924)
Gustav Mahler (1860–1911)
Sergei Rachmaninov (1873–1943)

20th CENTURY

Leoš Janáček (1854–1928)
Claude Debussy (1862–1918)
Richard Strauss (1864–1949)
Jean Sibelius (1865–1957)
Ralph Vaughan Williams (1872–1958)
Arnold Schoenberg (1874–1951)
Maurice Ravel (1875–1937)
Béla Bartók (1881–1945)
Igor Stravinsky (1882–1971)
Sergei Prokofiev (1891–1953)
Aaron Copland (1900–1990)
George Gershwin (1898–1937)
Benjamin Britten (1913–1976)
Dmitri Shostakovich (1906–1975)
Olivier Messiaen (1908–1992)
Witold Lutoslawski (1913–1994)

20th – 21st CENTURY MODERNS

Karlheinz Stockhausen (1928–2007)
György Ligeti (1923–2006)
Harrison Birtwistle (1934–)
Arvo Pärt (1935–)
Steve Reich (1936–)
Kaija Saariaho (1952–)
Judith Weir (1954–)

JAZZ

Edward Kennedy 'Duke' Ellington (1899–1974)
Louis Armstrong (1901–1971)
William James 'Count' Basie (1904–1984)
Billie Holiday (1915–1959)
Ella Fitzgerald (1917–1996)
Thelonious Monk (1917–1982)
John Birks 'Dizzy' Gillespie (1917–1993)
Charles Mingus (1922–1979)
John Coltrane (1926–1967)
Miles Davis (1926–1991)
Herbie Hancock (1940–)
Wynton Marsalis (1961–)

MUSICAL THEATRE

Jerome Kern (1995–1945)
Irving Berlin (1888–1989)
Cole Porter (1891–1964)
Richard Rodgers (1902–1979)
Stephen Sondheim (1930–)
Andrew Lloyd Webber (1948–)

FILM

Max Steiner (1888–1891)
Scott Bradley (1891–1977)
Bernard Herrmann (1911–1975)
Ennio Morricone (1928–)
Jerry Goldsmith (1929–2004)
John Williams (1932–)
Hans Zimmer (1957–)

Index

TO OUR PARENTS, FOR THE GIFT OF MUSIC, AND TO ALL
OF YOU WHO PASS ON THIS GIFT – THROUGH TUITION
AND SUPPORT – TO THE NEXT GENERATION. – M.B. & R.B.

MEURIG AND RACHEL BOWEN live and work in Gloucestershire, England. Rachel teaches singing and class music, and conducts a number of children's choirs. Meurig is Director of the Cheltenham Music Festival.

DANIEL FROST is an award-winning illustrator and graduate of the Royal College of Art. His work blends modern images with traditional mediums. He lives and works in Copenhagen and London.

Quarto is the authority on a wide range of topics.
Quarto educates, entertains and enriches the lives of
our readers—enthusiasts and lovers of hands-on living.
www.quartoknows.com

First published in Great Britain in 2017 by Wide Eyed Editions
an imprint of Aurum Press, 74–77 White Lion Street, London N1 9PF
QuartoKnows.com • Visit our blogs at QuartoKnows.com

The School of Music copyright © Aurum Press Ltd 2017
Illustrations copyright © Daniel Frost 2017
Text copyright © Meurig and Rachel Bowen 2017

ISBN 978-1-84780-860-8

The illustrations were created digitally • Set in Gill Sans and Daniel Frost
Designed by Nicola Price • Edited by Jenny Broom • Published by Rachel Williams
Printed in Dongguan, Guangdong, China
1 3 5 7 9 8 6 4 2

MIX
Paper from
responsible sources
FSC® C104723

MUSIC SAMPLES

Many thanks to the following musicians who have specially recorded demonstrations of their instruments and voices.

LESSON 6:
INSTRUMENTS THAT YOU PLUCK
Avi Avital (mandolin)
Andrew Cronshaw (Kantele, Guzheng)

LESSON 7:
INSTRUMENTS THAT YOU BLOW
Jess Gillam (saxophone)
Christian Lindberg (trombone)
Eddie Parker (flute)
The Tibetan Monks of Tashi Lhunpo
Monastery (long horns)
Tigran Aleksanyan (duduk)

LESSON 8:
INSTRUMENTS THAT YOU HIT
Evelyn Glennie (percussion)
Cheltenham Community
Gamelan Players (gamelan)

LESSON 9:
INSTRUMENTS WITH KEYS
Benjamin Nicholas (organ)
Eddie Parker (synthesizer)
Ksenija Sidorova (piano accordion)

LESSON 10:
INSTRUMENTS THAT YOU BOW
Nicola Benedetti (violin)
Sheku Kanneh-Mason (cello)

LESSON 11:
VOICES
Mary Bevan (soprano)
Sarah Connolly (mezzo-soprano)
James Gilchrist (tenor)
Bryn Terfel (baritone)

LESSON 13:
STRING QUARTETS
Carducci String Quartet

Nicola Benedetti and Sheku Kanneh-Mason featured courtesy of Decca Classics
Avi Avital, Ksenija Sidorova and Bryn Terfel featured courtesy of Deutsche Grammophon

Download a free QR code reader from your device's app store, then scan the code below to stream the music on your phone or tablet. Alternatively, you can visit schoolofmusic.online